BLACK HISTORY
Kids' Edition

Stephen Jones Sr.

PAGE PUBLISHING, INC.
New York, NY

First originally published by Page Publishing, Inc. 2015

ISBN 978-1-63417-890-7 (pbk)
ISBN 978-1-63417-891-4 (digital)

Printed in the United States of America

Contents

Mansa Musa (c. 1280–c. 1337) 11

Makeda (Queen of Sheba) 13

Hannibal (247–183 BC) 15

Hatshepsut (c. 1503–1482 BC) 17

Shaka (1818–1828) 19

Yaa Asantewa (c. 1840–1921) 21

Taharka (710–644 BC) 23

Dahia al-Kahina 25

Afonso I (1506–1540) 27

Amanirenas (ca. 40 BC–10 BC) 29

Tutankamun (c. 1341 BCE–c. 1323 BCE) 31

Nzinga (1582–1663) 33

Behazin (1844–1906) 35

Nefertiti (ca. 1370 BC–1330 BC) 37

Henry Christophe (1767–1820) 43

Ellen Johnson Sirleaf 45

Haile Selassie I 47

Kamehameha I 49

Vicente Guerrero 51

I remember as a young adult attending school, my least favorite subject was history. My favorite subject was science. Science was the subject that caught my interest right away. In fact, I would read science books instead of comic books. Now history, on the other hand, you couldn't get me to read a history book if there was a dollar bill and a candy bar after every page. I hated history, and I never did well in class early on. It just was so boring to me. If you ask me why, I would guess and say, there wasn't anything in the early history books that would capture my attention. I would lose focus after a short period.

Today, it is my favorite subject by far. I try to learn and understand history as often as possible. I am so heavy into history, people ask me all the time, "Why aren't you a history professor?" In fact, some of my close friends call me Professor.

I'm not sure of the exact sudden change; however, I believe it was when I started college at Long Beach State. Although I grew up in the San Francisco Bay Area (Berkeley and Oakland), I went to college in Long Beach. Long Beach State had an excellent black history program. I am very blessed to have attended because it changed my life and the way I view life.

Let's discuss why.

Keep in mind, this book is written with young kids in mind. I am writing an adult version, which will go far in detail. Adults, by the way, please feel free to enjoy and entertain yourself. In fact, I encourage you to read along with your kids and friends and family members as well.

Let's now discuss the term *black history*. To understand the term, you have to break it down into two words: *black* and *history*. Let's start with *black*.

The word *black* can be used as an adjective, a noun, or a verb. These are not my words and have been taken directly out of a dictionary.

Let's give two examples of *black* as an adjective according to the dictionary.

1. Of the very darkest color owing to the absence of or complete absorption of light; the opposite of white: *black smoke, her hair was black.*
2. Of any human group having dark-colored skin, esp. of African or Australian Aboriginal ancestry: *black adolescents of Jamaican descent.* Of or relating to black people: *black culture.*

Let's now give two examples of *black* as a noun according to the dictionary.

1. Black color or pigment: *a tray decorated in black and green, a series of paintings done only in grays and blacks.*
2. A member of a dark-skinned people, esp. one of African or Australian Aboriginal ancestry: *a coalition of blacks and whites against violence.* (also *Black.*)

Finally, let's now give two examples of *black* as a verb according to the dictionary.

1. Make black, esp. by the application of black polish: *blacking the prize bull's hooves.*
2. Make (one's face, hands, and other visible parts of one's body) black with polish or makeup, so as not to be seen at night or, esp. formerly, to play the role of a black person in a musical show, play, or movie: *white extras blacking up their faces to play Ethiopians.*

The reason I emphasize on the term *black history* is because some people are insulted when they are categorized as blacks. I won't go far into detail; however, I will point out a few things.

First of all, if someone is insulted when they are called or categorized as black, they have every right to be. If anyone is insulted when they are called a word they are not comfortable with, they have the right to prefer to be considered a term of their liking. Please understand that. I will even take it a little further. When I hear the word *black*, the very first thing that comes to mind is the color black. I don't consider it being a nationality until it is used in that term. That goes the same for any color. Colors are often used to determine the status of belonging to a particular nation. This can be very confusing. Sometimes it can be insulting. Sometimes one color can be associated with many nations that are extremely far apart in distance.

Personally, I consider myself as a black man. I also consider myself as an African American. I don't have a problem with either. To go a little further, taking everything into account, I am comfortable with simply being called American. To take it where it needs to be, let's all use the term *human being*.

Don't get me wrong, this is how I see it. I am not trying to insult anyone. You have the right to your own opinion. The reason I am trying to make a point here is black history should be called history. It should be included and accepted and understood by everyone. It should not be exclusive to only one month per year, and it should be studied worldwide. If black history or any ethnic group history is not included in our history books, then we are not educating the world properly. We are also missing out on so much knowledge and information.

Now let's discuss the word *history*. The word *history* is used as a noun. Let's give a few examples of how *history* is used according to the dictionary.

1. The study of past events, particularly in human affairs: *medieval European history.*
2. The past considered as a whole: *letters that have changed the course of history.*
3. The whole series of past events connected with someone or something: *the history of Aegean painting.*
4. A continuous, typically chronological, record of important or public events or of a particular trend or institution: *a history of the labor movement.*

Now that we have a better understanding of the term *black history*, let's have some fun discovering history that is extremely hard to find. We are going to be learning about kings and queens of Africa, leaders, presidents, generals, and most importantly, history.

There will be plenty of paintings and artwork. Some of the paintings are a representative or a portrayal and even a hypothesis. These particular paintings are an educated guess or a well-put-together opinion. Some of the great people in this book do not have any photographs, paintings, or any way of knowing exactly what they look like. For that reason, on a few of the paintings, don't judge the paintings, saying, "I don't think this is how this person looked."

Instead look at the paintings and embrace the history behind the great leader he or she stands for. Some dates cannot possibly be accurate because the time frame is so long ago that information is not available.

Once again, we are not trying to insult anyone.

We went to great measures (based on the information at hand) to create the best portrayals possible. That being said, enjoy, have a good time, and always share your knowledge.

Mansa Musa
(c. 1280–c. 1337)

Mansa Musa was the emperor of the wealthy Mali Empire. *Mansa* is translated as *king* or *emperor*. When you think of Mali, you can't think of it being a wealthy nation. When you think of rich, you think Bill Gates. If you compared Mansa Musa's wealth to today's standards, Mansa Musa would be worth four hundred billion dollars. That's right, $400,000,000,000. I bet you didn't see that number popping up. He was a very rich king.

Mansa Musa, a devout Muslim, was well known across Northern Africa and the Middle East. He is known for his incredible hadj, a holy pilgrimage to Mecca. He led thousands of people on a caravan across the Sahara from Mali to Mecca and back. During which, he spent and gave away to the poor so much gold it depressed its value over twelve years. He was a scholar and a great businessman. He made Gao and Timbuktu part of his empire. At the time, Timbuktu had one of the finest and most prestigious universities in the world. The Mali Empire included most of West Africa. Word of the Mali Empire traveled all the way across the Mediterranean into Europe.

MAKEDA

12

Makeda (Queen of Sheba)

Queen Makeda was a ruler of Ethiopia. Some stories state that Sheba was located in modern-day Saudi Arabia while some books refer to Sheba as being part of Ethiopia. Her story can be found in the Bible, the Quran, the Kebra Nagast, Yemeni and Ethiopian history. We believe the story in the Kebra Nagast to be the most accurate. In all accounts, we know she was a very wealthy and powerful queen. The imperial family of Ethiopia claims they are the direct offspring of Makeda and King Solomon. It is said King Solomon and Makeda had a son together. His name is Menelik I. He later became the first emperor of Ethiopia.

Despite Makeda being so rich, she gave King Solomon tons of gold. One of the most controversial stories in history is how the Ark of the Covenant came to Ethiopia with Menelik I. The Ark of the Covenant is a gold-plated chest. According to many, it contains the Ten Commandments.

HANNIBAL

Hannibal
(247–183 BC)

Hannibal, ruler of Carthage, was one of the greatest generals to date. Carthage is modern-day Tunisia. His tactics are still studied by army leaders all over the world today. He was the best military strategist in history. His armies included African war elephants and Numidians. Numidians were master horsemen. They were from present-day Algeria. Hannibal invaded Italy for fifteen years. He also conquered major portions of Spain.

HATSHEPSUT

Hatshepsut
(c. 1503–1482 BC)

Hatshepsut, pharaoh of Kemet, was one of the most successful Egyptian pharaohs. She built a great navy, and her national defense was extraordinary. Although she was very successful in warfare, her era was considered to be peaceful. She was great on international relations and foreign trade.

In one of her famous expeditions to the land of Punt. Her ships returned with ivory, gold, leopard skins, ebony, incense, and myrrh trees. Her building projects could not be rivaled by any other culture for one thousand years. Hatshepsut's temple is only one example of her remarkable accomplishments. She built magnificent temples and restored many while the Egyptian economy flourished.

Some say Hatshepsut is the most powerful and most successful woman of power of all time.

SHAKA

Shaka (1818–1828)

Shaka, king of the Zulus, united ethnic groups in South Africa against colonial rule. He has been called a military genius. He revolutionized warfare by using special tactics and standardized weaponry. He is credited for introducing new weapons and new fighting styles. He invented a shorter spear with a longer blade (iklwa), which was used in close quarters and a longer spear (assegai) for long-range attack. He also invented heavier shields made of cowhide of different colors to distinguish different warriors within the army. He taught his army mobility and tactical weapons technique that were far more advanced than his opponent. His army intimidated enemies to the point they would flee at first sight of them.

YAA ASANTEWA

Yaa Asantewa (c. 1840–1921)

Yaa Asantewa, queen mother of Ejisu of the Ashanti Empire. The story about her battle against British colonialists is a big part of the history of Ghana.

When their king was taken by the British, the chiefs had a meeting discussing about how to rescue him and force the enemy out. Some chiefs did not want to engage in war, and some were afraid. Yaa Asantewa was present at the meeting.

She was so frustrated and upset, she stood up and said, "Now I have seen that some of you fear to go forward to fight for our king. If we were in the brave days of Osei Tutu, Okomfo Anokye, and Opoku Ware, chiefs would not sit down to see their king taken away without firing a shot. No white man could have dared to speak to chief of the Ashanti in the way the governor spoke to you chiefs this morning. Is it true that the bravery of the Ashanti is no more? I cannot believe it. It cannot be! I must say this: if you, the men of Ashanti, will not go forward, then we will. We, the women will. I shall call upon my fellow women. We will fight the white men. We will fight till the last of us falls in the battlefields."

Taharka
(710–644 BC)

Taharka, pharaoh of Egypt and king of the kingdom of Kush, ruled the largest empire in ancient Africa. He became king of not only Kush but Kemet as well. He combined military campaigns in Western Asia and led expeditions to Spain. He also fought the Assyrians in defense of Israel. He saved Jerusalem.

This is huge for Hebrew history and world history for that matter. His campaigns can be found in the Bible.

He started a building program that included some of the most magnificent and majestic building projects ever. The numbers were phenomenal. Despite his conflicts with the Assyrians, this was a prosperous era for his kingdom.

He is also known as the last pharaoh.

DAHIA AL-KAHINA

Dahia al-Kahina

Dahia al-Kahina, queen of Mauritania, fought off the Arabian army against invasion and drove them north into Tripolitania. She formed a united front against invaders, which was a resistance to Arab expansion in the region. This was very effective.

AFONSO I

Afonso I
(1506–1540)

Afonso I, king of the Kongo, is responsible for a very successful school system in Africa. Some say he modernized Africa with education, carpentry, agriculture, masonry, and politics. He was the first king to resist the slave trade.

Afonso I attempted to convert Kongo to Catholic. He wanted to merge his religious traditions with Christianity. He built schools for boys and girls and also sent young boys to study in Portugal. His son was one of them and became bishop in 1518. He served in Kongo in the early 1520s.

Although Afonso's conversion is unclear, the Portuguese had something different in mind. They were more interested in slavery. Afonso wrote many letters including two to the king of Portugal about the violence and destabilization the slave traders were the cause of. In the end, what he thought was a good and peaceful thing to do turned out to be a devastation.

AMANIRENAS

Amanirenas
(ca. 40 BC–10 BC)

Amanirenas, kandake of Kush, led her army against the Romans. Kandake, Candace, or Queen Mother all refer to queen. Queen Amanirenas was one of the greatest kandakes. She went to battle with the Romans, who took over Egypt after Cleopatra VII's death. The war lasted five years. During one battle, the Kushites attacked the Romans in Egypt and defeated them in Philae and Syene and drove the Jews from Elephantine Island. They returned to Kush with prisoners, loot, and treasures of war including statues of Emperor Augustus.

These battles went back and forth until a peace treaty was finally reached. Queen Amanirenas is remembered as being brave, courageous, and fearless.

TUTANKAMUN

Tutankamun
(c. 1341 BCE–c. 1323 BCE)

Tutankamun, pharaoh of Egypt, is one of the best known pharaohs partly because of the discovery of his tomb, which was found nearly intact. It was almost untouched by thieves. His tomb drew irresistibly the attention and interest of the world. He has become history's most famous royalty.

Tutankamun's, also known as King Tut, original name was Tatankhaten. He changed his name to Tutankamun in honor of the god Amun. He was eight or nine years of age when he became king and died only ten years later. The cause of his death is unknown.

His father, Akhenaten, wanted the Egyptians to believe in one god (Aten). While Tutankamun was king, he restored traditional beliefs. He was more in tune with traditional beliefs and the god Amun.

NZINGA

Nzinga
(1582–1663)

Nzinga, queen of Ndongo and Matamba, was educated in hunting, archery, diplomacy, and trade.

She led many battles and peace treaties with both the Portuguese and the Dutch. The Portuguese betrayed her several times. Their interest was to capture as many Mbundu as possible and sell them as slaves. The Portuguese advanced to the Ndongo territory and captured thousands of Ndongo as well.

Despite Nzinga's efforts as she formed an alliance with other communities and became allies with the Dutch, the Portuguese tried their best to destroy the Mbundu culture. She resisted the Portuguese, personally leading her troops into battle.

BEHANZIN

Behazin
(1844–1906)

Behazin Hossu Bowelle, king of Dahomey, was also known as the King Shark. He established a well-trained army, which included fifteen thousand men and five thousand women. This superior army was one of the most powerful throughout West Africa.

In 1882, France declared a protectorate over Porto Nova without permission. By 1885 they occupied the entire coastal strip. Behazin army fought against the French occupation. Later a treaty was signed.

France continued to occupy Cotonou; however, Behazin made them pay for the use of the port.

In 1894, he was defeated by French forces. Behazin, not wanting his people to be massacred, surrendered himself. He thought he would meet with the president of France to sign an agreement for his country. The French tricked him. Instead of going to France, he was exiled to Martinique, where he was treated as a war prisoner.

Behazin once said, "You can remove a man from his country, but you can never remove his country from a man's heart or erase a great man from history."

NEFERTITI

Nefertiti
(ca. 1370 BC–1330 BC)

Nefertiti, queen of Kemet (Ancient Egypt), was the wife of Pharaoh Akhenaten. Nefertiti means "the beautiful one has arrived." Although Cleopatra gets all the Hollywood credit, there is not any evidence that states Cleopatra was beautiful. Also, Cleopatra ruled Egypt when it was in ruins.

Nefertiti is known for her beauty, power, and loyalty to her husband. She is portrayed as equal to her husband and displayed in a way other Egyptian queens were not. Nefertiti and Akhenaten ruled Egypt during one of the wealthiest periods in Ancient Egyptian history. They originated monotheism (the belief of one god).

Nefertiti is often shown with a crown of a pharaoh. There are also depictions of her in battle. She took on roles only a pharaoh would. Her bust is one of the most widely recognized symbols.

These kings and queens are random picks and are not in any particular order. There are many other leaders that we could have easily added and should be studied or at least talked about. As we have acknowledged, there were famous kings and queens all over the entire continent of Africa. These kings and queens were not only exclusive to Egypt. The fact of the matter is, there were black kings and queens all over the world. We will be observing some of these famous leaders later.

I wanted to share more history on more black leaders of the past; however, I also want to share some of the great leaders of the more present. Also I want to move around the globe more. You see, blacks, Moors, Olmecs, Egyptians, Polynesians, Chinese, Vikings, West Africans, and many other cultures traveled the world far before Columbus did.

In fact, when Columbus found America, there were many, many cultures living together in harmony and peace. There were many cultures from all over the globe that had settled and made the so-called New World home. These people were not Indians (the title they were all given). They didn't even all look alike. There were many different cultures. There were many different religions and beliefs. Some had dark skin; some had light skin. Some had yellow skin; some had red skin. How could you classify them all as Indians, unless you were lost and thought you were in India? After all, there were even people in America who wore turbans and long clothing similar to the way some modern-day Muslims dress.

So don't just remember African history as Egyptian history. There is so much history just south of Egypt in Sudan, which was once Nubia. Over 250 pyramids were constructed in Nubia (modern-day Sudan), and not one is studied in history books. The kingdom of Kush is not studied in schools. Could this be because these people were undoubtedly black Africans?

You see, for some strange reason (probably white supremacy), only the history from North Africa or the slave trade in West Africa is ever mentioned. In fact, I want you to check this out. Pay careful attention to this clause. This is taken directly from an employee self-identification survey. This is not a small-time company but rather a huge organization. It reads as follows:

"White (not of Hispanic or Latino origin): All persons having origins in any of the original peoples of Europe, North Africa, or the Middle East."

Do you see what's going on here. Since when are people of North Africa white? How about the Middle East? If we go by this scenario, when my great-grandkids grow up and they ask, was Jesus black or white, his or her teachers will respond, if Jesus was from the Middle East, then he would have had to be white. You see what's happening now. This will be the same issue for King Tut, Hannibal, Moses, the Moors, and countless factors. In fact, all these people I mentioned have already been portrayed as white. This is an effort to say all good things are white. The problem with this is many people, even black, actually believe this nonsense. The world has been brainwashed. Some people think that if you want to know how the Ancient Egyptians would have looked in the past, then look at Egyptians today. This is so far from the truth. That would be like saying the indigenous people from America must have looked like Justin Bieber and Miley Cyrus. The Egyptians today are invaders. They have come from many regions and are not indigenous to Egypt or Africa, for that matter.

Now let's talk about the effects of this ongoing problem. If you strip a man's history, he doesn't know where he is coming from, so he could not possibly know where he is going. He has lost respect for his people, his culture, his family, his family values, his beliefs, and even himself. This, I believe, is done deliberately. You and others may say, "What's the problem? We have a black president, we have black millionaires, we have black-owned businesses, we even have black networks." Well, we have always had black presidents (kings).

We have always had black millionaires. Mansa Musa in today's time would be worth four hundred billion dollars. There are not too many people that want you to know about him. Hatshepsut was one of the greatest leaders of all time. Yet in the United States, we haven't even considered a woman president.

Right now, there needs to be a time for change. The black man is not respected in the United States by any other culture. Cultures have come to the United States with the notion that blacks are violent, drug addicts, criminals, lazy, and ignorant. It doesn't help when we prove them right at times. What these other cultures aren't told is there are unprivileged people all over the globe. They come in all shapes, sizes, and colors.

In fact, the same countries they have come from face the same problems and sometimes worse.

One of our biggest problems in the United States is the incarceration rate of black Americans. The numbers are staggering. Some of the crimes committed do not even deserve the punishment. You have people serving time for possession of a small amount of marijuana, which arguably should be legal. It is a proven fact that marijuana is less harmful than alcohol. Look at what happens: You lose your right to vote. You can't serve as a juror. You can't own a firearm. You can't leave the state. You are branded in the workplace. In a way of looking at it, you have become a slave. They say slavery is over; however, that is far from the truth. Another problem with incarceration is the waste of a human's mind and body. How can you rehabilitate someone if he is locked up in a cell twenty-three hours a day? What are you teaching them? They have become comfortable with not doing anything all day. It would be a better situation if they brought back the chain gang. It sounds terrible; however, at least a person isn't locked up all day and may even learn the challenges of hard work.

Time is important and should not be wasted.

To other cultures, despite what you have seen on television, black people are kind, courteous, fun to be around, respectful, and very intelligent. We have been dealt a bad hand. Blacks have been at times so courteous that we have been taken advantage of. We were tricked into slavery and have never recovered. We were tricked into drug abuse and have never recovered. We are hated by the world for no apparent reason. Although unappreciated, we are the most copied culture in the world. Everybody wants to be us, but nobody wants to be us.

Now it's time so check out some more great leaders of the world. Once again, these fabulous people are picked at random. Please enjoy.

HENRY CHRISTOPHE

Henry Christophe
(1767–1820)

Henry Christophe, president of the state of Haiti, was born into slavery. He was a key leader in the Haitian Revolution. He fought alongside L'Ouverture against the French. In 1802, L'Ouverture was captured and was deported to France. The war continued, and the Africans won their independence in 1804. They distinguished themselves in history to be the first independent black republic in the West.

In 1807, Christophe was elected president and proclaimed Haiti a republic nation. He had himself proclaimed Henry I, king of Haiti.

Christophe constructed many palaces including Citadelle Laferrière and Sans-Souci Palace. He is known for economic development in Haiti. He transformed a slave-based economy into a productive nation of newly freed people. Haiti had become a nation of great wealth.

ELLEN JOHNSON SIRLEAF

Ellen Johnson Sirleaf

Ellen Johnson Sirleaf is the twenty-fourth and current president of Liberia. She is the world's first elected black female president. She also is the first elected head of state in Africa. She was born in Monrovia, Liberia, and received several degrees from colleges in the United States (including Harvard).

Ellen Johnson Sirleaf, also known as Iron Lady, is an African icon. She won the Nobel Prize for peace in 2011 for promoting Liberian reconciliation, nonviolent struggle for the safety of women, and women's rights. She stands for peace and women's rights. She is known for her personal financial integrity. Liberia, although in need of a strong infrastructure, has enormous resources. The large petroleum companies are attracted as well as foreign investors.

Today Ellen Johnson Sirleaf continues to win award after award and continues to demonstrate passionate commitment to hard work and the importance of education.

HAILE SELASSIE I

Haile Selassie I

aile Selassie, emperor of Ethiopia, is a defining figure in both Ethiopian and African history. He is said, by some, to be the heir to King Solomon and Queen Makeda. He is also referred as the Conquering Lion of the tribe of Judah, Jah Rastafari, King of Kings, Elect of God, the Power of Authority, the Author of Mankind. He was one of the world's best-known legends. At his fortieth anniversary, representatives of a hundred nations came to salute the authority of this great leader. He won the respect of the world.

This is one of his many quotes:

"Throughout history, it has been the inaction of those who could have acted, the indifference of those who should have known better, the silence of the voice of justice when it mattered most, that has made it possible for evil to triumph."

KAMEHAMEHA I

Kamehameha I

Kamehameha I, king of Hawaii, conquered the Hawaiian Islands. He was also known as Kamehameha the Great. He united the Hawaiian Islands into one kingdom in 1810. He was a great leader and a courageous warrior. His unification of Hawaii was an extraordinary achievement. Without this unification, the islands may have been torn apart by foreign interest.

Every year, on June 11, Kamehameha Day is celebrated as a public holiday in the state of Hawaii. Floral parades are held throughout the state. Kamehameha's statues (one at Kapa`au, Kohala, on the Island of Hawaii; another in front of Ali`iolani Hale, a building in downtown Honolulu; and another in Hilo, Hawai`i, the Big Island) are draped in fresh leis. A celebration is also held in the United States Capitol, where a replica of the famous stands in Statuary Hall weighing fifteen thousand pounds. There are also statues in Maui and Las Vegas.

VICENTE GUERRERO

Vicente Guerrero

icente Guerrero, president of Mexico, abolished slavery in 1829, forty years before Lincoln did the same in the United States. He was the leading general in the Mexican war for independence. Between 1810 and 1821, Guerrero won 491 battles. He fought against Spain for independence as a revolutionary general and later became president of Mexico.

The Mexican state of Guerrero and Vincent Guerrero in Baja, California, are two of several towns named in his high respect.

> A free state protects the arts, industry, science and trade; and the only prizes virtue and merit: if we want to acquire the latter, let's do it cultivating the fields, the sciences, and all that can facilitate the sustenance and entertainment of men: let's do this in such a way that we will not be a burden for the nation, just the opposite, in a way that we will satisfy her needs, helping her to support her charge and giving relief to the distraught of humanity: with this we will also achieve abundant wealth for the nation, making her prosper in all aspects.
>
> —Vicente Ramón Guerrero Saldaña,
> speech to his compatriots

hope you have enjoyed the material shared with you so far. The last five spectacular world leaders are of modern era, and in fact, one of which is still in power today (Ellen Johnson Sirleaf). All of the famous individuals mentioned are some of my favorite heroes. There are countless others—so many it would take quite a long time to list. I want you, the reader, to go out and seek the history that is missing from us. I guarantee your favorite heroes won't be the same as mine. Also study and research the names mentioned in this book. Because of lack of concrete evidence, some facts may be arguable, especially the dates that go so far back in time no archaeologist has an answer. It is for that reason I purposely left out some dates.

I don't think it is as important to know what date a person was born or what date they reigned than it is to know what they accomplished. Once again, research, study, and share information so we can all be educated and enlightened.

I have a small list you can get started with when you are ready to research more great leaders: Nelson Mandela, Luisa Diogo, Queen Charlotte, Queen Lydia Liliuokalani, Toussaint L'Ouverture, and Barack Obama.

So now let me tell you our history is likely to have a profound effect on success, survival, and well-being. Life, after all, does not start on an even playing field. If you think it does or if you think it doesn't matter, take a look at the following pictures.

Which one of these houses would you prefer residing, growing up as a young adult? I take it you picked the first one. Even though they both have advantages and disadvantages, I think the first one may be a little easier to survive the consequences of the environment.

Take a look at the next two photos. I strongly believe that there is a place intended for the occupants of the house of far less value.

Cover design: Joseph Sutherland
Artwork: Gwendolyn McShepord
Artwork Copyright: Pineal Gland Entertainment®

About the Author

Stephen Jones has always enjoyed seeking and sharing knowledge. If we can't share knowledge with each other we are wasting precious time in the advancement of the world. He is writing an adult version of this book. It will go further in depth and it will have social issues as well. This will be a must read. He's tired of everyone pointing fingers and blaming everyone else for their current situation when a big part of the blame is looking right at them when they look in the mirror. Now Stephen is aware some people are born into devastation and their condition is overwhelming. He's going to be addressing people who have a very easy solution to their problems. The answers are right in front of them. Look out for "Black History Adults Edition".